Recipe Hacks for Cheese Puffs

About the Author

Laura Sommers is **The Recipe Lady!**

She is the #1 Best Selling Author of over 80 recipe books.

She is a loving wife and mother who lives on a small farm in Baltimore County, Maryland and has a passion for all things domestic especially when it comes to saving money. She has a profitable eBay business and is a couponing addict, avid blogger and YouTuber.

Follow her tips and tricks to learn how to make delicious meals on a budget, save money or to learn the latest life hack!

Visit her blog for even more great recipes and to learn which books are **FREE** for download each week:

http://the-recipe-lady.blogspot.com/

Visit her Amazon Author Page to see her latest books:

amazon.com/author/laurasommers

© Copyright 2017. Laura Sommers.
All rights reserved.
No part of this book may be reproduced in any form or by any electronic or mechanical means without written permission of the author. All text, illustrations and design are the exclusive property of
Laura Sommers

About the Author ii

Introduction 1

Broccoli with Cheese Curls...2

Cheetah Marshmallow Treats 3

Spicy Cheese Curl Marshmallow Treats 4

Caramel Coated Cheese Curls...5

Chocolate Covered Cheese Curls 7

Cheetah Pork Chops...8

Cheese Puff Chicken 9

Hot Cheetah Chicken 10

Cheese Puff Mozzarella Sticks...11

Peanut Butter, Cheese Curls and Jelly 12

Macaroni and Cheese Puff Cheese Pie 13

Cheese Curls Crust Quiche..14

Cheese Puff Meatballs 16

Cheesy cheese Curls Burger 17

Cheetah Sushi Roll 18

Cheese Curl Log 20

Cheese Puff Spinach and Potato Frittata..21

Spicy Cheese Curl Ramen..22

Cheese Curls Spaghetti and Meat Sauce..23

Spicy Cheese Curls Kale Salad 24

Cheetah Popcorn 25

Cheetah Grilled Cheese..26

Cheese Puff Asparagus and Mushroom Frittata 27

Cheese Curls Bagel	28
Cheese Curl Nachos	29
Cheese Curl Pizza	30
Cheetah Jalapeno Poppers	31
Cheetah Bacon	32
Cheetah Skins	33
About the Author	34
Other Cookbooks in This Series	35

Introduction

Cheese puffs are one of America's favorite snacks. They can be called cheese puffs, cheese curls, cheese balls or puffed cheese snacks. They come in regular, spicy and white cheddar varieties. Some snacks are puffed and some are a thinner and less buffed for a more crunchy texture.

Cheetos are the mose popular brand for cheese puffs but other snack company's such as Herr's and Lays also make their own version.

Cheese puffs, with their cheesy crunchy texture make a perfect ingredient for many foods as a coating or a secret ingredient. This recipe book contains lots of recipes for you to try that use cheese puffs as an ingredient. Cheese puffs are delicious but they don't have to be boring if you know how to Hack It!

Broccoli with Cheese Curls

Ingredients:

2 cups heavy cream
3 tbsp. minced garlic
2 tbsp. minced shallots
6 whole black peppercorns
1 bay leaf
1 1/2 cups grated aged Gouda
1/2 cup grated Parmesan
Kosher salt, to taste
1 1/4 lb. (about 2 large heads) broccoli, cut into small florets
3 tbsp. extra-virgin olive oil
1 tsp. crushed red chile flakes
2 cups original cheese curls, crushed by hand

Directions:

1. Make the cheese sauce: Heat cream, 2 tbsp. garlic, shallots, peppercorns, and bay leaf in a 2-qt. saucepan over medium-high heat.
2. Cook, stirring often, until reduced by half, about 6 minutes.
3. Remove pan from heat, stir in cheeses until melted, and season with salt.
4. Set a fine strainer over a small saucepan and strain sauce, discarding solids. Set aside and keep warm.
5. Bring a large pot of salted water to a boil over high heat.
6. Add broccoli and cook, stirring, until crisp-tender, about 3 minutes.
7. Drain broccoli, transfer to a bowl of ice water, and let chill.
8. Drain and transfer to paper towels to dry; set aside.
9. Heat oil in a 12" skillet over medium-high heat.
10. Add remaining garlic and chile flakes and cook until fragrant, 1 minute.
11. Add broccoli and cook, stirring often, until just subtly browned, about 6 minutes.
12. To serve, spoon cheese sauce evenly among 6 warm serving bowls or small plates.
13. Top sauce with broccoli and a generous sprinkling of cheese curls. Serve immediately.

Cheetah Marshmallow Treats

Ingredients:

2 bags (7 oz. each) crunchy cheese curls
3 Tbsp unsalted butter
1 (10 oz.) bag miniature marshmallows

Directions:

1. Lightly spray a 7×11-inch baking dish; set aside.
2. Open a bag of cheese curls to let the air out. Scrunch the opening back up to close, then crushed the bags to break up the cheese curls in roughly smaller pieces. Repeat with the second bag then set aside.
3. In a large sauce pan, melt the butter. Once melted, add the marshmallows and continue to heat over medium low heat, stirring constantly until the marshmallows are completely melted and smooth. Immediately, and quickly, stir in the two bags of cheese curls. Continue to gently mix until the marshmallows are evenly distributed.
4. Transfer immediately to the prepare baking dish and press to evenly spread. Let cool, then cut into squares.

Spicy Cheese Curl Marshmallow Treats

Ingredients:

2 9-oz. bags spicy cheese curls
3 tbsp. butter
10 1-oz. bags miniature marshmallows

Directions:

1. Spray an 8×8 pan with cooking spray and set aside.
2. Melt marshmallows and butter in a heated saucepan, then add to spicy cheese curls.
3. Mix well.
4. Pour the mixture into a 8×8 pan.
5. Spread the mixture using your hands.
6. Set for 1 hour.
7. Enjoy.

Caramel Coated Cheese Curls

Ingredients:

2 (8oz.) white Cheddar cheese curls
1 cup butter
2 cups light brown sugar, packed
1/2 cup light corn syrup
1/2 tsp salt
1/2 tsp baking soda
1/2 tsp cream of tartar
1/2 tsp vanilla
Tools needed
Very large roasting pan
3 qt. or larger saucepan (nothing smaller)
Silicone spatula (best for separating the cheese puffs)

Directions:

1. Combine the butter, brown sugar, corn syrup, and salt in the 3 qt saucepan.
2. Melt the butter first then add the corn syrup, brown sugar, and salt.
3. Bring to a boil while stirring constantly.
4. At first the ingredients will be in two distinct layers.
5. As it boils, it will combine together.
6. When it does, stop stirring and let it boil for 2 minutes.
7. The mixture will hold air bubbles and increase in volume.
8. Pour the cheese curls into the pan. If your work surface is cold, put the pan on a towel or potholders.
9. This will prevent the heat from the pan from dissipating too quickly. Preheat the oven to 250 degrees F.
10. After two minutes of boiling without stirring, remove from heat.
11. Add the baking soda, cream of tartar, and the vanilla.
12. Word of caution with the vanilla, try and sprinkle it in and stir immediately.
13. If you add it quickly and do not stir right away, the vanilla will travel to the bottom of the saucepan and immediately boil.
14. The vapor generated will rush to the surface and you could get a small explosion of molten sugar.
15. Mix well. The color will change to a lighter shade.
16. Quickly pour the caramel onto the cheese curls.
17. Pour the whole thing on and try to cover the whole surface.

18. Do not attempt to pour in gradually while mixing or the coating will be uneven.
19. Using the silicone spatula, mix the cheese curls and caramel.
20. Put the pan into the oven and bake for 1 hour, mixing every 15 minutes.
21. The coating will even out.
22. Take the pan out of the oven after 1 hour of baking and mixing.
23. Mix gently as it cools.
24. Use the spatula to separate large clumps.
25. As it cools, the caramel will harden and the cheese curls should not stick together.
26. If you wait too long before mixing and the cheese curls harden into clumps, put it back in the oven for 10 to 15 minutes.
27. Do not try to force them apart when it is cool or they will crack and crush.

Chocolate Covered Cheese Curls

Ingredients:

1 (9 oz.) pkg. cheese curls
1 (12 oz.) pkg. semisweet chocolate morsels

Directions:

1. Open your bags of chips and put them in a bowl or on a plate so that they will be easy to reach for when you're ready to dip. Line a baking sheet with parchment paper and set to the side.
2. In a double boiler, melt the chocolate morsels over low heat until melted, stirring frequently to prevent scorching.
3. When melted, remove from heat.
4. Dip the cheese curls in the chocolate so that about 3/4 of the snack is covered.
5. Tap against the side of the pan to allow excess chocolate to drip off.
6. Place on the prepared parchment-lined sheet.
7. Repeat with the remaining cheese curls.
8. Sprinkle with sprinkles if desired.
9. Let the chocolate coated chips set for about two hours.

Cheetah Pork Chops

Ingredients:

4 pork chop cutlets
1 egg
Cheese curls, crushed fine
Japanese breadcrumbs

Directions:

1. Beat the eggs.
2. Mix cheese curls and bread crumbs together in a shallow bowl.
3. Heat oil over medium high heat until hot.
4. Dip the pork chops one at a time, first in the egg, then dredge through the cheese curls-bread crumb mix.
5. Put in pan.
6. Cook for about 2 minutes on one side then flip the chops over.
7. Cook until done on the other side.
8. Try to only flip once.

Cheese Puff Chicken

Ingredients:

3 cups crunchy cheese puffs
1/3 cup parmesan cheese, grated
1/4 cup flour
1/2 tsp. salt
1 egg
1 tbsp. water
2 boneless skinless chicken breasts

Directions:

1. Place the cheese puffs in your food processor and process into small crumbs.
2. Add the Parmesan cheese and pour onto a plate.
3. Coat chicken breasts in flour & salt.
4. Combine egg & water. Beat until well combined.
5. Dip floured Chicken in egg mixture.
6. Coat the chicken in the crumbs.
7. Place on a lightly greased baking sheet.
8. Bake for 35-45 minutes at 350 degrees F until chicken is cooked through.

Hot Cheetah Chicken

Ingredients:

Chicken
Bag of spicy cheese curls
Buttermilk
Cayenne pepper, optional
Hot sauce, optional

Directions:

1. Place chicken into a glass bowl.
2. Sprinkle chicken with cayenne pepper or hot sauce.
3. Pour buttermilk over chicken until fully coated.
4. Let chicken marinate in the refrigerator for 2 to 8 hours.
5. Crush spicy cheese curls.
6. Place in a bag and roll with a rolling pin to crush.
7. Pour crushed cheese curls on a plate.
8. Pour out buttermilk and rinse the chicken.
9. Coat both sides of the chicken in the crushed cheese curls.
10. Heat oil or warm up the oven, depending on cooking method chosen.
11. If you are frying the chicken, heat oil in deep fryer to 325 degrees F.
12. If frying, place in heated oil for a few minutes until done.
13. If baking, preheat oven to 375 degrees F.
14. Bake about 25-35 minutes until done.
15. Cook until internal temperature is 165 degrees F.

Cheese Puff Mozzarella Sticks

Ingredients:

1 cup bread crumbs
1 1/2 cups spicy cheese puffs
2 eggs
1 pkg. mozzarella cheese sticks
Vegetable oil
Salt

Directions:

1. Blend bread crumbs and spicy cheese puffs together in a food processor until fine and mixed. Pour the mixed crumbs into a medium-sized bowl.
2. Crack eggs into a small bowl and beat them. Set bowl aside.
3. Unwrap the mozzarella cheese sticks. Cut each in half so it's easier for you to roll them in the beaten egg and batter.
4. Dip and roll each cheese stick into the beaten egg and then drop the sticks into the crumb bowl.
5. Roll each cheese stick into the crumbs until fully coated. For convenience, use a spoon with your separate hand so that bread crumbs don't build up on your fingers.
6. Repeat steps 4 and 5 with all cheese sticks if you want a thicker crust.
7. Pour vegetable oil into a skillet and set on medium heat. Add some salt so that you will not get burned by spatters.
8. Using metal tongs, carefully drop a cheese stick into the heated oil.
9. Leave on each side of about 5 seconds.
10. Serve with your favorite dipping sauce.

Peanut Butter, Cheese Curls and Jelly

Ingredients:

2 slices of sandwich bread
1 tbsp. peanut butter, crunchy or smooth
1 tbsp. jelly of choice
1/2 cup Cheese curls

Directions:

1. Spread the peanut butter evenly on one slice of bread.
2. Spread the jelly on the other slice of bread.
3. Place Cheese curls on the peanut butter side of the bread, using the peanut butter to help the Cheese curls slick to the bread.
4. Lay the jelly coated piece of bread on top for the peanut butter and Cheese curls side with the spreads sandwiched in between.
5. Serve and enjoy!

Macaroni and Cheese Puff Cheese Pie

Ingredients:

2 cups shredded Cheddar cheese
1 cup uncooked macaroni
2 1/4 cups milk
4 eggs
1/2 cup baking mix (such as Bisquick)
1/4 tsp. salt
1/4 tsp. red pepper sauce
1/4 cup shredded Cheddar cheese
1/2 cup crushed cheese curls

Directions:

1. Heat oven to 400 degrees.
2. Grease pie plate 10 x 1 1/2 inches.
3. Mix 2 cups cheese and the macaroni. Sprinkle in plate.
4. Beat remaining ingredients except 1/4 cup cheese until smooth, 15 seconds in blender on high or 1 minute with hand beater.
5. Pour into plate.
6. Bake until knife inserted in center comes out clean about 40 minutes. Sprinkle with 1/4 cup cheese and cheese curls.
7. Bake until cheese is melted, 1 to 2 minutes.
8. Cool 10 minutes.

Cheese Curls Crust Quiche

Ingredients:

Pie Crust Ingredients:

2 cups cheese curls, crushed fine
1/3 cup melted butter
1 egg white, lightly beaten with 1 tsp water

Pie Crust Directions:

1. Put cheese curls crumbs in large bowl.
2. Add beaten egg, mix thoroughly.
3. Let the melted butter cool below 150 degrees, then add melted butter and mix thoroughly so the butter is evenly distributed.
4. Press evenly into pie pan (don't grease the pan) to make firm, even layer throughout.
5. Blind bake @ 300°F for 8 – 10 minutes or until firm.
6. Cool before filling.

Quiche Ingredients:

1 pie crust (above)
2 tbsps. (1/4 stick) butter
2/3 cup chopped shallots (about 3 medium)
4 to 5 cups sliced/chopped assorted mushrooms (such as chanterelle, stemmed shiitake, oyster, crimini, and button; 12 to 14 oz.)
4 large eggs
1 cup half and half
1/2 tsp. salt
1/2 tsp. freshly ground black pepper
1/2 tsp. freshly grated or ground nutmeg
1 1/2 cups (packed) coarsely grated Gruyere cheese (about 7 oz.), divided

Quiche Directions:

1. Preheat oven to 450 degrees F.
2. Melt butter in heavy large skillet over medium-high heat. Add shallots; sauté until beginning to soften, about 2 minutes.

3. Add mushrooms; sprinkle with salt and pepper and sauté until mushrooms are tender and beginning to brown, about 8 minutes. Transfer to plate; spread out to cool slightly.
4. Whisk eggs, half and half, milk, 1/2 tsp. salt, 1/2 tsp. pepper, and nutmeg in large bowl to blend.
5. Stir in 1 cup Fontina cheese and sautéed mushrooms.
6. Pour filling into crust. Sprinkle remaining 1/2 cup cheese over quiche.
7. Bake quiche until puffed, golden brown, and just set in center, about 45 minutes.
8. Cool 30 minutes. Cut into wedges.

Cheese Puff Meatballs

Ingredients:

1 lb of spicy italian sausage
1 lb of ground beef
2 eggs
1 cup crunchy cheese puffs, crushed
1/2 tsp salt
1/4 tsp pepper
2 tbsp. Italian seasoning
2 garlic cloves minced

Directions:

1. Preheat oven to 350 degrees F.
2. Combine all ingredients in bowl, mix well and roll into balls.
3. Place in large dish.
4. Bake in 350 degree oven for 25 minutes or until cooked through.
5. Serve and enjoy!

Cheesy cheese Curls Burger

Ingredients:

½ lb 80/20 fresh ground chuck/beef patties (never frozen)
1 cup of your favorite cheese sauce
4 cups of cheese puffs (regular or spicy)
4 burger buns
Salt and pepper
Olive oil or cooking oil
Jalapeños, optional

Directions:

1. Season patties with salt and pepper on both sides. Heat cast iron skillet to medium heat.
2. Add 1 tbsp. of oil to skillet and cook patties to desired temperature.
3. Toast each bun in the oven on broil top and bottom.
4. Add cheese sauce to both sides of the buns top and bottom.
5. Add patty to the bun with cheese sauce and top it with crunchy cheese curls
6. Add jalapeños to add spice if desired.

Cheetah Sushi Roll

Ingredients:

2 tbsp. crab mix
1 cup sushi rice
1 oz. cucumber, jullienned
1 tsp sriracha
3 slices avocado
1 tsp spicy mayo
½ sheet pink soy paper
Spicy cheese puffs, whole
Spicy cheese puffs, crushed
1 oz. wasabi cream
8 jalapeno, paper thin slices
8 oz. cream cheese

Crab Mix Ingredients:

8 oz. cooked crab meat
8.8 oz. imitation crab meat
4 tbsps. Kewpie mayo

Spicy Mayo Ingredients:

1/2 oz. chili oil
1 oz. Japanese 7 Spice (Togarashi) powder
1/2 oz. Tabasco
1/2 oz. sriracha
1 btl (17.6 oz.)Kewpie Japanese mayo
1/2 oz. sesame oil

Wasabi Cream Ingredients:

1/2 cup sour cream
1 tsp wasabi
1/4 red bell pepper, chopped
1/4 green bell pepper, chopped

Directions:

1. On a clean, dry cutting board, place the soy paper on top of your bamboo matt (wrap your bamboo mat in plastic wrap first) with the long side closest to you.
2. Spread the rice evenly to cover the entire soy paper.
3. Flip the soy paper over so the rice side is facing down and the soy paper side facing up.
4. With the long side still closest to you, arrange the avocado first, then cucumber, cream cheese, about 3-4 four whole cheese curls.
5. Add Sriracha and spicy mayo on top and then place some crab mix on the bottom third of paper. Make sure not place the crab mix too close to the edge because when you roll it the mix will ooze out the ends.
6. With your thumb, lift the edge of the bamboo mat that's closest to you. With your fingers keeping the filling in place, roll the edge of the paper away from you so that it just slightly tucks under the filling.
7. Continue to roll the paper into a tight cylinder, making sure there are no air pockets, removing the mat as you go
8. The seam should be on the bottom.
9. Place the bamboo mat (which is still wrapped in plastic wrap) over the roll and shape into a squarish roll. Make sure ends are tucked in so the roll doesn't fall apart when you cut it.
10. Remove bamboo mat.
11. Place crushed cheese puffs in shallow bowl, pan or plate large enough to accommodate the roll. Pick up the roll and press the roll into the crushed cheese puffs on all sides, leaving you a nice red roll.
12. Place roll on a plate and slice equally using a sharp knife.
13. Arrange your pieces on a plate and drizzle with wasabi cream and garnish with the thinly sliced Jalapenos.
14. Mix well all the crab mix ingredients in a large bowl and chill.
15. Mix well all ingredients for the spicy mayo mix in a large bowl.
16. Pour into a squeeze bottle and chill.
17. Mix all ingredients for the wasabi cream in a large bowl, pour into squeeze bottle and chill.

Cheese Curl Log

Ingredients:

8 oz. cream cheese, softened
5 oz. cheese curls, finely crushed
4 oz. Pimento stuffed olives, chopped into small pieces

Directions:

1. In a bowl, blend the cream cheese, half the cheese curls, and the chopped olives.
2. Mix thoroughly.
3. Place on wax paper and roll into a log.
4. Roll the log in the remaining crushed cheese curls.
5. Garnish with more cheese curls halved lengthwise and sliced pimento stuffed olives.

Cheese Puff Spinach and Potato Frittata

Ingredients:

1 cup crushed cheese puffs
2 tbsps. olive oil
6 small red potatoes, sliced
1 cup torn fresh spinach
2 tbsps. sliced green onions
1 tsp. crushed garlic salt and pepper to taste
6 eggs
1/3 cup milk
1/2 cup shredded Cheddar cheese

Directions:

1. Heat olive oil in a medium skillet over medium heat.
2. Place potatoes in the skillet, cover, and cook about 10 minutes, until tender but firm.
3. Mix in spinach, green onions, cheese puffs and garlic.
4. Season with salt and pepper.
5. Continue cooking 1 to 2 minutes, until spinach is wilted.
6. In a medium bowl, beat together eggs and milk.
7. Pour into the skillet over the vegetables.
8. Sprinkle with Cheddar cheese and more cheese puffs.
9. Reduce heat to low, cover, and cook 5 to 7 minutes, or until eggs are firm.

Spicy Cheese Curl Ramen

1 pkg. Ramen noodles, beef flavored
1 small bag spicy cheese curls

Directions:

1. Cook Ramen noodles according to package directions and include the flavor packet.
2. Break up the cheese curls slightly and add to the noodle soup before serving.
3. Enjoy!

Cheese Curls Spaghetti and Meat Sauce

Ingredients:

1 pkg. dried spaghetti
1 jar pasta sauce
1 lb. ground beef or chuck
1 bag of spicy cheese curls
Grated parmesan cheese, optional

Directions:

Cook spaghetti according to package directions.
Cook the ground beef in a saucepan until brown and crumbly.
Drain, but leave in the pan.
Pour spaghetti sauce in with the beef and cook until hot, 5 minutes.
You can add the cheese curls to the beef now or lay them on top when serving.
Put spaghetti on serving plates or bowls.
Add meat sauce.
If you did not add the cheese curls to the meat sauce before, layer them on top.
Sprinkle grated parmesan cheese on top.
Serve and enjoy!

Spicy Cheese Curls Kale Salad

Ingredients:

3/4 cup spicy cheese curls
1 tbsp. white wine vinegar
Juice of a lemon
3 tbsps. extra-virgin olive oil
Kosher salt
1 bunch kale, rinsed, stemmed, and shredded
1/3 cup chopped toasted walnuts
1/4 cup finely grated parmesan cheese
1 Pink Lady apple

Directions:

1. Pulse the spicy cheese curls in a food processor until they're the texture of panko breadcrumbs.
2. Whisk together the white wine vinegar, juice of half a lemon, olive oil, and a good pinch of salt in the bottom of a mixing bowl.
3. Add the kale, and massage the dressing into each leaf.
4. Add the walnuts and parmesan cheese, and toss to coat.
5. Core and thinly slice the apple, and toss with the rest of the lemon juice in a small bowl. Add the apple and any juices to the salad.
6. Top the salad with spicy cheese curls crumbs, and serve.

Cheetah Popcorn

Ingredients:

1 bag microwave popcorn
1 bag cheese puffs, any variety

Directions:

1. Pop popcorn according to package directions.
2. Pour in to a bowl.
3. Crush the cheese puffs. It is okay to leave some larger pieces.
4. Mix cheese puffs with popcorn, especially the dust created when crushed.
5. Toss together.
6. Serve and enjoy!

Cheetah Grilled Cheese

Ingredients:

2 slices of thick bread
Butter
1 tsp. Italian seasoning
Slices of Cheddar cheese
Cheese curls

Directions:

1. Heat a skillet over medium high heat.
2. Put a couple of tbsps. of butter in a bowl.
3. Sprinkle the Italian seasoning in with the butter and mix until combined.
4. Butter one side of one slice of bread with the seasoned butter.
5. Add a bit of plain butter to the skillet.
6. Place the bread with the butter mixture in the skillet, butter side down.
7. Add slices of Cheddar cheese.
8. Add a layer of cheese curls.
9. Thickly butter one side of the other piece of bread with the butter mixture.
10. Carefully lay the other piece of bread on top of the sandwich in the pan, butter side up.
11. Cook for about two minutes on this side.
12. Flip the whole thing over in one flip using a large spatula.
13. Cook for 2-3 minutes on the other side.
14. Serve with pickles and more cheese curls.

Cheese Puff Asparagus and Mushroom Frittata

Ingredients:

1 cup cheese puffs, crushed, plus more for top
1 tbsp. butter
3 tbsps. olive oil
1/2 pound fresh asparagus, trimmed and cut into 1 inch pieces
1/2 pound fresh mushrooms, sliced
6 eggs
1 tbsp. water
1 tsp. chopped fresh thyme
3 tbsps. freshly grated Parmesan cheese
1/2 cup shredded mozzarella cheese

Directions:

1. Preheat oven to 325 degrees F (165 degrees C).
2. Melt butter in an oven-safe skillet over medium heat.
3. Stir in olive oil and asparagus, and cook until the asparagus is tender, about 10 minutes.
4. Stir in the mushrooms, and continue cooking about 5 minutes.
5. In a medium bowl, whisk together eggs, water, cheese puffs and thyme.
6. Pour into the skillet, and reduce heat to low.
7. Cover, and cook 5 minutes.
8. Transfer the skillet to the preheated oven.
9. Bake 10 to 15 minutes, until eggs are no longer runny.
10. Top the mixture with Parmesan cheese and mozzarella cheese and more crushed cheese curls.
11. Turn on the broiler, and broil until cheeses are melted and lightly browned.

Cheese Curls Bagel

Ingredients:

1 bagel, sliced in half
Cream cheese
Cheese curls, any flavor

Directions:

1. Smear cream cheese on one half or the sliced bagel.
2. Lay cheese curls down on top of the cream cheese.
3. Place the other half of the bagel on top to create a bagel sandwich.
4. Serve and enjoy!

Cheese Curl Nachos

Ingredients:

Cheese curls
Shredded Mexican cheese blend
Jalepenos, sliced
Black olives, sliced
Sour cream for serving
Guacamole for serving

Directions:

1. Lay a layer of cheese curls on a microwavable safe plate.
2. Layer the rest of the ingredients on top.
3. Heat in the microwave until the cheese is melted in 10 second bursts.
4. Serve with sour cream and guacamole.

Cheese Curl Pizza

Ingredients:

1 can or pkg. pizza dough
1 jar pizza sauce
Shredded Mozzarella or pizza cheese blend
Italian seasoning
Cheese curls
Jalapeño slices, optional
Pepperoni, optional
Slice mushrooms, optional
Sliced black olives, optional
Other pizza toppings, optional

Directions:

1. Prepare the pizza dough according to package directions.
2. Spread a layer of pizza sauce over the dough.
3. Sprinkle Italian seasoning on top.
4. Spread a layer of cheese on top.
5. Layer on cheese curls.
6. Layer on other toppings.
7. Bake according to package directions.
8. Serve and enjoy!

Cheetah Jalapeno Poppers

Ingredients:

4 strips bacon, cooked and chopped
1/2 cup chopped pimientos or roasted red pepper
6 oz. cream cheese
1 cup shredded smoked gouda
1/2 cup shredded sharp cheddar
1 dash cayenne pepper
1 dash paprika
8 jalapeños, stemmed, cut lengthwise, and with the seeds removed
1/2 cup flour
Salt and pepper, to taste
2 eggs
2 tbsps. milk
5 cups cheese puffs, ground in a food processor
Oil, for frying

Directions:

1. Make the filling by combining the first seven ingredients.
2. Stuff the jalapeño halves with the filling and place on a baking sheet lined with parchment.
3. Set up three bowls. In the first, mix together flour with a pinch of salt and a few cracks of pepper.
4. In the second, beat the eggs with the milk, a pinch of salt, and a few cracks of pepper.
5. In the third, place the cheese puff crumbs.
6. Coat the stuffed peppers in flour, the egg mixture, and then the cheese puff crumbs.
7. Deep fry at 365 degrees F for two minutes each or bake at 350 degrees F for 30 minutes.

Cheetah Bacon

Slices of bacon
Eggs
Flour
1 bag of spicy cheese curls
BBQ sauce for serving

Directions:

1. Heat oil in a skillet.
2. Crush the cheese curls in a food processor.
3. Put crushed cheese curls in one bowl.
4. Wisk the eggs in another bowl.
5. Put flour in a third bowl.
6. Dip the bacon in the three bowls in this order: flour, egg, cheese puff crumbs.
7. Place bacon in the hot oil and fry until crisp.
8. Drain on paper towels.
9. Serve with BBQ sauce.
10. Serve and enjoy!

Cheetah Skins

Ingredients:

4 large baking potatoes
1 cup cheese puffs, crushed
2 tsps. olive oil
2 tsps. salt
1 tbsp. butter
4 cloves minced garlic
1 1/2 cups shredded Cheddar cheese
1/2 cup sour cream
1/4 cup chopped green onion, divided
Ground black pepper to taste
4 slices cooked bacon, crumbled
1 pinch paprika, or to taste

Directions:

1. Preheat oven to 425 degrees F (220 degrees C).
2. Rub potatoes with olive oil and salt; pierce each several times with a fork and arrange onto a baking sheet about 6 inches apart.
3. Bake in preheated oven until easily pierced with a fork, 50 to 60 minutes.
4. Remove from oven and set aside to cool until cool enough to handle, keeping oven heat at 425 degrees F (220 degrees C).
5. Halve potatoes lengthwise and scoop potato from each half into a bowl, leaving about 1/4 inch of the potato attached to the skin all the way around.
6. Melt butter in a large saucepan over medium-high heat.
7. Saute garlic in butter until fragrant, 1 to 2 minutes.
8. Stir scooped potato, cheese, cheese puffs, sour cream, and most of the green onion together with the garlic and butter; cook and stir the mixture until heated and smooth, about 5 minutes.
9. Scoop the potato mixture into the potato skins and arrange onto the baking sheet.
10. Sprinkle more crushed cheese puffs on top.
11. Bake in oven until heated through, 15 to 20 minutes.
12. Garnish with remaining green onion, bacon, and paprika.

About the Author

Laura Sommers is **The Recipe Lady!**

She is the #1 Best Selling Author of over 80 recipe books.

She is a loving wife and mother who lives on a small farm in Baltimore County, Maryland and has a passion for all things domestic especially when it comes to saving money. She has a profitable eBay business and is a couponing addict, avid blogger and YouTuber.

Follow her tips and tricks to learn how to make delicious meals on a budget, save money or to learn the latest life hack!

Visit her blog for even more great recipes and to learn which books are **FREE** for download each week:

http://the-recipe-lady.blogspot.com/

Visit her Amazon Author Page to see her latest books:

amazon.com/author/laurasommers

Other Cookbooks in This Series

- **Recipe Hacks for Saltine Crackers**
- **Recipe Hacks for Canned Biscuits**
- **Recipe Hacks for Canned Soup**
- **Recipe Hacks for Beer**
- **Recipe Hacks for Peanut Butter**
- **Recipe Hacks for Potato Chips**
- **Recipe Hacks for Oreo Cookies**
- **Recipe Hacks for Pasta Sauce**
- **Recipe Hacks for Canned Tuna Fish**

May all of your meals be a banquet
with good friends and good food.

Made in the USA
Middletown, DE
11 October 2024

62429226R00024